CULTURAL DIVERSITY
AND
ECONOMIC EDUCATION

CULTURAL DIVERSITY
and
ECONOMIC EDUCATION

Elias H. Tuma and Barry Haworth

PACIFIC BOOKS, PUBLISHERS
Palo Alto, California

Library of Congress Cataloging-in-Publication Data

Tuma, Elias H.
    Cultural diversity and economic education / Elias H. Tuma and Barry Haworth.
       p.   cm.
    Includes bibliographical references.
    ISBN 0-87015-264-5
    1. Economics. 2. Economics—Social aspects. 3. United States—
Economic conditions. 4. United States—Social conditions. 5. Economics—
Study and teaching. I. Haworth, Barry, 1958-
II. Title.
HB171.5.T78   1993
330—dc20   93-24504
                                                   CIP

PACIFIC BOOKS, PUBLISHERS
P.O. Box 558, Palo Alto, California 94302-0558, U.S.A.

*To all those who believe that education
is the best protection against discrimination*

PREFACE

Economic behavior is influenced by many factors including tradition, race, ethnicity, and gender and so are solutions to economic problems facing the economy as a whole and its individual sectors. Therefore, understanding and explaining these influences should aid in policy making and implementation. Economic discrimination against racial, ethnic, and gender groups apparently persists today at the expense of these groups and the aggregate economy. Yet very little is said about these issues in economics textbooks and introductory economic education. In bringing these issues to the attention of educators and students, we hope to make economic education more relevant and applicable to business and to policy making. *Cultural Diversity and Economic Education* is intended as a supplement to introductory textbooks to provide points of departure for economic analysis of cultural diversity and economic discrimination. Its ultimate value will depend on the willingness of educators and their students to focus more directly on these issues than they have done in the past.

We are grateful to Anne Mayhew and an anonymous reader for their valuable comments and suggestions. We thank the Teaching Resources Center of the University of California, Davis, for financing this study. We also thank the staff of the Department of Economics at the University of California at

Davis, especially Donna Raymond, for taking charge of typing and producing the numerous drafts of the manuscript. Special thanks also go to Henry and Romayne Ponleithner for their cooperation in publishing and copyediting the book.

Davis, California   ELIAS H. TUMA
January 1993   BARRY HAWORTH

CONTENTS

LIST OF TABLES

CULTURAL DIVERSITY
AND
ECONOMIC EDUCATION

1

INTRODUCTION

Interest in cultural diversity is on the rise, partly because of increasing sensitivity to cultural differences and special group rights, and partly because of policy makers' increasing awareness of the relevance of cultural differences in designing policies and implementing programs. Economists have been rather slow to recognize the need for differentiation among culturally diverse groups and specification and detail in designing economic education. Furthermore, they rarely seem to recognize the importance of cultural diversity and pluralism in explaining economic behavior. In most cases, economics courses are designed on the assumption that the population is homogeneous, uniformly rational, market oriented, and a maximizer, especially in material terms. The fact that different ethnic, cultural, and gender groups may have different tastes and behave differently in response to changes in incomes, prices, interest rates, or other institutional dynamics, or that such multipatterned behavior warrants variable policy measures has rarely been taken into consideration.

For example, it is known that the unemployed, the poor, and the homeless are concentrated in certain locations; it is also known that they come mostly from certain segments of the population. If so, would not the treatment of unemployment, poverty, and homelessness be more efficient if those locations or population segments were carefully targeted by policy makers? National fiscal and monetary policies that treat these problems indirectly through trickle-down effects are slower, costlier, and less dependable than selectively targeted but directly implemented policies. The national approach has been tried and its effects have not been satisfactory, as the data on persistent poverty, unemployment, and homelessness in the United States indicate.

The fact that different segments of the population have different fertility rates, family sizes, and life expectancies makes data on national per capita incomes, family incomes, and national per capita expenditure on health, education, and welfare of little use in targeting problems of unemployment, undertraining, poor health, and deprivation.

The assumption that the market is blind to color, ethnicity, and sex makes it equally blind to the special problems faced by the groups thus differentiated. Furthermore, the fact that the market is imperfect limits the usefulness of any policy that depends largely on the market in trying to eliminate the problems faced by these groups. On the contrary, the market approach may perpetuate and aggravate the income, educational, and welfare inequalities among ethnic and gender groups. In a sense, the market tends to be biased against these groups, which have been marginalized over time by forces of the market. In such cases, economic policies directed against ethnic and gender discrimination may be more effective if they circumvent the market for given periods of time rather than depend on it. Some observers, including economists, have tended to blame "culture" or "ethnic affiliation" for the economic ills of the members of those cultural or ethnic groups. To what extent is "blaming the victim" a legitimate explanation of economic deprivation or privilege?[1]

From these observations it may be concluded that a differentiated policy that takes into consideration the cultural, ethnic, racial, and gender composition of the population would be more efficient (less costly and more effective in reaching the constituents) than a blanket application of one policy to all segments of the population. Furthermore, it may be more efficient to target policies and apply controlled intervention in the market than to depend fully on the imperfect and color-sex-blind market.

These arguments are not new. One industry, the advertising industry, has already made use of them. Political parties and politicians also have used them. Both political parties and advertising agencies have long tailored their programs to address different audiences differently. Public agencies have often devised special programs to cater to certain groups, but these programs are usually considered exceptions, deviations from the norm and from the basic principles of economics. We propose that economists and economic policy makers would do well to pay more attention to the racial, ethnic, cultural, and gender diversities of the population, and to design multiple fiscal and monetary policies to deal with the specific problems faced by these various groups. We propose further that such policy differentiation should be integrated in economic education beginning in introductory courses, as intended by this publication, which is offered as a supplement to introductory textbooks in economics.

The significance of cultural diversity in the study of economics will be demonstrated by discussing a number of topics primarily from the standpoint of macroeconomics, though both discussion and topics should be relevant to the micro course as well. The number of topics discussed is kept small to avoid overburdening the regular course. Each topic will be treated in a separate chapter to make possible partial and selective use of this Supplement. The data presented may not be current or comprehensive, but they should be sufficient to illustrate the points made in each topic. On the other hand, we challenge students to update the information and to supplement it with data relating to the specific cultural groups or issues in which they may be particularly interested. We also encourage students to keep a data bank on the issues that interest them for future reference and analysis.

The text in this Supplement is intended to provoke discussion, from the cultural diversity perspective, of economic principles and policies regarding major issues facing the economy.

It is not intended to replace the textbook or to explain the main concepts fully. These concepts should be explained in the context of the course before economic discrimination is discussed.

The underlying hypothesis of our discussion is that the teaching of economic theory and policy in the United States and elsewhere has tended to oversimplify by concentrating on the economics of homogeneous populations, perfect markets, uniform populations of consumers, producers, savers, investors, employers, workers, etc., regardless of the diversity of their ethnic, racial, cultural, or gender, interests, attitudes, preferences, and behaviors, or the constraints they face.

Similarly, economic policy making has tended to oversimplify by assuming that uniform fiscal and monetary policies apply equally to all segments of the population and that all are rational maximizers and decision makers. That the objects of rationality and the components of the utility objective function may vary from one cultural group to another, or that certain groups may face market barriers beyond their control that limit their mobility and freedom of choice has seldom been treated in principles textbooks and curricula.

Furthermore, while less government may be more efficient than more government in certain circumstances, as stipulated by standard economic analysis, the opposite may be true in some situations. For example, this has been true in dealing with economic problems of the ghetto, high unemployment, runaway inflation, and other crisis situations, including those in which minorities and women have been the victims.

We should emphasize, however, that cultural diversity is significant to all ethnic and gender groups, whether minority or majority, not only to those who are disadvantaged and discriminated against. Cultural diversity relates to those who suffer from underendowment because of limited education, underutilization because of under-employment or unemployment, and underrewarding because of lower compensation, as well as to those groups that seem to be privileged, such as Asians, Jews, Northern and Western Europeans, Arabs, etc.[2] These latter groups tend to enjoy a disproportionate share of acquired endowment, utilization, and rewarding. Therefore, the need to recognize cultural diversity goes beyond dealing with the disadvantaged. It relates equally to higher efficiency, better-quality product, and higher quality of life for all. Our emphasis, however, will be on the disadvantaged, the groups that have the most potential for growth and improvement, both for themselves and for the economy, because they represent wasted capacity and unrealized potential output for the economy as a whole. The effects of underendowment, underutilization, and underrewarding may be technically illustrated by reference to a production possibility frontier. All three forms of deprivation prevent individuals and groups from producing at the frontier; often they bring the frontier itself closer to the origin.

To facilitate the discussion, each chapter contains illustrative data, relevant economic principles, and policy implications. In addition, it suggests issues for student investigation and discussion. The topics to be covered are:

1. Demographic and Economic Profile of the Population: Racial, ethnic, and gender composition of the population, and variable fertility, infant mortality, and life expectancy; the distribution of income, wealth, employment versus unemployment, and level of education among these groups.

2. Group Diversity and Consumer Behavior: Patterns of expenditure by ethnic and gender groups, and the expected responses to changes in consumer prices, income changes, and fiscal and monetary policy.

3. Saving and Investment: Diversity of behavior among savers, investors, and active participants in the market by race, ethnicity, and sex; potential responses to fiscal and monetary policy, especially changes in interest rates, credit availability, and changes in the market.

4. Poverty, the Underclass, and Economic Policy: What can economists do about them?

5. Economic Discrimination: Discrimination as a chronic source of waste; private and social benefits and costs; policy successes and failures.

6. Other Economic Issues.

2

DEMOGRAPHIC AND ECONOMIC PROFILE
OF THE POPULATION

Economic policy and analysis usually assume a homogeneous population. Little attention is paid to cultural, racial, ethnic, or gender differences as a matter of simplification to facilitate analysis, and it is assumed that differences between groups tend to offset each other and, therefore, that generalizations to the whole population are possible. To what extent are such assumptions justified and what effects do they have on economic policy? If these assumptions are realistic and harmless, the profiles of the subgroups in the population should be fairly similar to each other and to the profile of the population as a whole. Otherwise the differences cannot be ignored. Let us look at the facts.

From Table 2-1 it appears that the white population exceeds 80% of the total, though it is composed of various ethnic groups, all of which are Caucasian, such as Italian, Greek, Arab, East Indian, Irish, German, Slavic, etc. The blacks, Hispanics, Native Americans, and Asians (1980) receive a smaller percentage of income than their proportionate size in the population and lower median weekly wages than that of the majority. All four groups are overrepresented among the unemployed and families in poverty. They are underrepresented in the higher incomes per family, higher incomes per capita, and enrollment in college (except for Asians). Life

TABLE 2-1
DEMOGRAPHIC AND ECONOMIC PROFILE OF THE POPULATION: 1980, 1985, 1990[a]

	Total Population			White			Blacks			Native Americans			Hispanics			Asian/Pacific Islanders		
	1980	1985	1990	1980	1985	1990	1980	1985	1990	1980	1985	1990	1980	1985	1990	1980	1985	1990
% of Population[1]	100.0	100.0	100.0	85.9	84.9	80.3	11.8	12.1	12.1	0.6	0.7	0.8	6.5	7.5	9.0	1.7	2.3	2.9
% of Income[2]	100.0	100.0	100.0	89.8	90.0	89.0	6.4	7.5	7.8	0.3	-	-	3.3	4.6	5.0	1.4	-	2.6
Unemployment Rate[3]	6.5	7.2	5.5	5.7	6.2	4.7	11.8	15.1	11.3	13.2	-	-	8.9	10.5	8.0	4.7	-	4.2
% of Families in Poverty[4]	9.6	11.4	10.7	6.6	9.1	8.1	26.4	28.7	29.3	23.8	-	-	21.3	25.5	25.0	10.6	-	11.0
% of Net Wealth[5]	-	100.0	100.0	-	95.2	95.2	-	2.8	2.9	-	-	-	-	2.2	2.7	-	2.0	1.9
Income per Capita[6]	12,077	13,941	14,991	13,142	14,773	15,906	7,539	8,658	9,396	7,642	-	-	7,589	8,371	8,778	11,741	12,984	13,984
Income per Family[7]	38,213	41,701	44,447	40,352	43,513	46,406	25,999	27,037	28,714	27,647	-	-	28,567	29,306	30,544	43,977	53,324	53,112
Median Weekly Wage[8]	432	434	432	443	449	445	351	351	343	-	-	-	343	341	320	-	-	427
% Completing under 8 years of School[9]	10.2	7.5	6.2	7.7	6.5	5.4	19.9	14.8	11.1	16.4	-	-	32.2	29.0	27.2	12.7	-	9.7
% Completing College[10]	16.2	19.4	21.5	17.4	20.0	22.2	8.4	11.1	11.5	7.8	-	-	7.6	8.5	9.7	33.3	-	39.1
% of Total College Enrolled[11]	100.0	100.0	100.0	83.5	82.5	81.1	9.4	9.0	8.9	0.7	0.7	0.7	4.0	4.5	5.4	2.4	3.3	3.9
Life Expectancy[12]	73.7	74.7	75.4	74.4	75.3	76.0	68.0	69.5	70.3	-	-	-	75.5	-	-	79.6	-	-
Infant Mortality[13]	12.6	10.6	9.8	11.0	9.3	8.1	21.4	18.2	18.6	13.2	9.1	9.0	-	8.6	8.5	6.6	6.1	5.0
Fertility Rate[14]	68.0	66.2	67.0	64.5	62.9	65.2	87.3	82.0	78.4	94.4	-	94.1	-	88.7	93.2	80.2	-	58.1
Annual Population Growth Rate: 1980-1989 (in %)[15]	-	-	1.0	-	-	0.8	-	-	1.5	-	-	2.2	-	-	3.6	-	-	6.5

TABLE 2-1 (continued)

[a] Some rows may not sum to 100% because of rounding and because Hispanics are also included in Whites, Blacks, etc. in 1985 and 1990 (unless noted). All dollar values are in constant 1991 dollars (deflated by the CPI: base year = 1991).

[1] Resident Population. Sources: U.S. Bureau of the Census *News Release:* CB91-215 (June 12, 1991), Table 1; *United States Population Estimates, by Age, Sex, Race and Hispanic Origin: 1989*, Tables 2 and C.

[2] Estimated from data in *Money Income of Households, Families and Persons in the United States: 1991*; and *The Asian and Pacific Islander Population in the United States: March 1991 and 1990*.

[3] Sources: *Employment and Earnings* (January 1991), Table 3; *Asian and Pacific Islander Population: March 1991 and 1990*, Table 11; *Statistical Abstract of the United States: 1988*, Tables 607-608; 1980 Census, *General Economic and Social Characteristics* (PC80-1-C1), Table 168.

[4] Sources: *Poverty in the United States: 1991*, Table 4; *Asian and Pacific Islander Population: March 1991 and 1990*, Table 8; 1980 Census, *General Economic and Social Characteristics* (PC80-1-C1), Table 171. Value for Asians is for "Other Races," which is approximately 72% Asian. Estimated from data provided in *Household Wealth and Asset Ownership: 1988 and 1984.* 1990 % is for 1988, and 1985 % is for 1984.

[5] % of the total net worth of all assets owned by households in the United States. Value for Asians is for "Other Races," which is approximately 72% Asian. Estimated from data provided in *Household Wealth and Asset Ownership: 1988 and 1984.* 1990 % is for 1988, and 1985 % is for 1984.

[6] In 1991 dollars. Value for Asians in 1985 is estimated from data on average monthly income per capita, provided in *Asian Americans: A Status Report.* Sources: *Money Income of Households, 1991*, Table B-19; *Asian and Pacific Islander Population: March 1991 and 1990*, Table 2. 1980 Census, *General Economic and Social Characteristics* (PC80-1-C1), Table 170.

[7] Mean income per family, in 1991 dollars. Values for Asians in 1985 and 1990 are estimated from data in *Asian Americans: A Status Report*, and Asian and Pacific Islander Population: March 1991 and 1990, respectively. Sources: *Money Income of Households, 1991*, Table B-6; *Money Income and Poverty Status of Families and Persons in the United States, 1985*; Table 3; 1980 Census, *General Economic and Social Characteristics*, Table 170.

[8] Median weekly wage of full-time and salary workers in 1991 dollars. Value for Asians in 1990 is estimated from data in *Asian and Pacific Islander Population : March 1991 and 1990.* Sources: *Employment and Earnings* (January 1991), Table 59; *Handbook of Labor Statistics* (Bulletin 2340), Table 41, *Statistical Abstract of the United States: 1981*, Table 681.

[9] Calculated for the population over 25 years of age. Value for Hispanics in 1990 is for 1988. Estimated from data in: *Asian and Pacific Islander Population: March 1991 and 1990, The Black Population in the United States: March 1991; Digest of Education Statistics: 1990 and 1987*; and 1980 Census, *General Economic and Social Characteristics.*

[10] Calculated for the population over 25 years of age completing 4 or more years of college. Estimated from data in: *Asian and Pacific Islander Population: March 1991 and 1990, Black Population: March 1991; Digest of Education Statistics: 1987;* and 1980 Census, *General Economic and Social Characteristics.*

[11] All values for Whites and Blacks do not include Hispanics. Source: *Digest of Education Statistics: 1990*, Table 190. 1990 % is for 1988, and 1985 % is for 1984.

[12] Value for Asians is a simple average of the life expectancies reported for Japanese, Chinese, and Filipinos in California in 1980 (*Population Bulletin*, October 1985). Values for 1990 are provisional. Sources: *Monthly Vital Statistics Report* (September 30, 1992), Table 7; *Vital Statistics of the United States, 1985* (Mortality, Part A), Table 6-3, and *1980* (Mortality, Part A), Table 6-3.

[13] Infant deaths per 1,000 live births. Values for Native Americans and Asians in 1990 are for 1988; all others are for 1989. Values for Asians estimated from data in sources. Sources: *Monthly Vital Statistics Report* (September 30, 1992), Tables 11 and 26; *Vital Statistics of the United States, 1988* (Mortality, Part A), Table 2-4, *1985* (Mortality, Part A), Tables 2-4 and 2-19, and *1980* (Mortality, Part A), Table 2.4.

[14] Live births per 1,000 women, ages 15-44. Values for Native Americans in 1980 and 1990 (1990 value is for 1988), and Asians in 1980 are estimated from data in *Fertility of American Women: June 1990; United States Population Estimates, by Age, Sex, Race and Hispanic Origin: 1980-1988; Advance Report of Final Natality Statistics, 1988* (August 15, 1990); *Vital Statistics of the United States, 1988* (Natality), *1985* (Natality), and *1980* (Natality).

[15] Average annual growth rate. Source: *United States Population Estimates, by Age, Sex, Race and Hispanic Origin: 1989*, Table A.

Source: Elias H. Tuma + Barry Haworth
CULTURAL DIVERSITY AND ECONOMIC EDUCATION (Calif. Pacific Books, 1993)

TABLE 2-2

DEMOGRAPHIC AND ECONOMIC PROFILE BY GENDER[a]

| | Total Population | | | | Whites | | | | Blacks | | | | Native Americans | | | | Hispanics | | | | Asian/Pacific Islanders | | | |
| | Males | | Females | | Males | | Females | | Males | | Females | | Males | | Females | | Males | | Females | | Males | | Females | |
	1980	1990	1980	1990	1980	1990	1980	1990	1980	1990	1980	1990	1980	1990	1980	1990	1980	1990	1980	1990	1980	1990	1980	1990
% of Population[1]	48.6	48.7	51.4	51.3	41.9	41.1	44.0	42.8	5.6	5.8	6.2	6.6	0.3	0.4	0.3	0.4	3.2	4.3	3.3	4.3	0.8	1.4	0.9	1.5
% of Income[2]	66.7	64.0	33.3	36.0	59.5	56.3	28.6	30.5	4.4	5.0	3.4	4.0	0.3	-	0.2	-	2.8	3.8	1.6	2.3	1.1	2.7	0.6	1.5
Unemployment Rate[3]	6.5	5.6	6.5	5.4	5.8	4.8	5.6	4.6	12.3	11.8	11.3	10.8	13.9	-	11.9	-	8.5	7.8	9.6	8.3	4.2	4.3	5.2	4.2
Participation Rate[4]	74.4	76.1	50.5	57.5	75.3	76.9	50.0	57.5	65.8	70.1	53.5	57.8	68.6	-	47.9	-	77.2	81.2	49.3	53.0	74.2	74.5	57.5	58.9
% of Professionals[5]	59.6	54.7	40.4	46.1	53.8	50.0	34.8	40.9	2.4	2.6	3.4	3.7	0.2	-	0.2	-	1.8	1.9	1.2	1.8	1.3	1.9	0.8	1.3
% of Medium-to Higher-Skilled Nonprofessionals[6]	52.7	50.6	47.3	49.5	45.6	45.2	40.0	43.0	3.4	3.8	4.1	5.0	0.2	-	0.2	-	2.8	3.5	2.2	3.0	0.7	1.2	0.8	1.3
% of Lower-Skilled and Unskilled Workers[7]	59.1	55.0	40.9	45.2	44.2	45.3	29.9	35.5	8.1	8.8	6.8	7.8	0.4	-	0.3	-	5.4	7.9	3.2	4.0	0.8	1.3	0.8	1.1
Income per Capita[8]	25,027	27,136	11,465	14,497	26,254	28,283	11,633	14,733	16,098	17,699	10,386	12,555	17,516	-	9,494	-	18,304	18,185	9,785	11,033	-	25,055	-	13,732
Median Annual Income[9]	20,175	21,145	8,709	10,493	21,560	22,059	8,900	10,750	12,965	13,408	7,738	8,678	13,339	-	7,028	-	15,022	14,036	7,832	7,848	19,515	21,206	11,066	12,307
% Completing under 8 years of School[10]	10.7	6.6	9.8	5.8	8.1	5.8	7.3	5.1	22.0	12.7	18.2	9.9	16.7	-	16.1	-	31.4	27.8	32.9	28.1	10.3	7.5	14.9	11.6
% Completing College[11]	20.1	24.4	12.8	18.8	21.7	25.4	13.6	19.3	8.5	11.4	8.3	11.6	9.3	-	6.4	-	9.4	12.0	6.0	8.1	40.4	43.2	27.0	35.5
% of Total College Enrolled[12]	48.0	45.4	52.0	54.6	40.5	37.2	42.9	43.9	3.9	3.5	5.5	5.4	0.3	0.3	0.4	0.4	2.0	2.4	2.0	2.9	1.3	2.0	1.1	1.9

TABLE 2-2 (continued)

aSome rows may not sum to 100% because of rounding and because Hispanics are included in Whites, Blacks, etc. in 1990 (unless noted). All dollar values are in constant 1991 dollars (deflated by the CPI: base year = 1991).

[1]Resident Population. Value for Native Americans in 1990 is for 1989. Sources: *The Asian and Pacific Islander Population in the United States: March 1991 and 1990*, Table A; *The Black Population in the United States: March 1991*, Table 1; *The Hispanic Population in the United States: March 1991*, Table 1; *United States Population Estimates, by Age, Sex, Race and Hispanic Origin: 1989*, Table C.

[2]Value for Asians in 1990 is for "Other Races," which is approximately 72% Asian. Estimated from data in *Money Income of Households, Families and Persons in the United States: 1989 and 1980 Census of Population, General Economic and Social Characteristics* (PC80-1-C1), Table 170.

[3]Sources: *Employment and Earnings* (January 1991), Table 3; *Asian and Pacific Islander Population: March 1991 and 1990*, Table 11; 1980 Census, *General Economic and Social Characteristics*, Table 168.

[4]Sources: *Employment and Earnings* (January 1991), Table 3; *Asian and Pacific Islander Population: March 1991 and 1990*, Table 11; 1980 Census, *General Economic and Social Characteristics*, Table 168.

[5]Managerial and Professional Specialty occupations as a % of Total Employed Professionals. Estimated from data in *Employment and Earnings* (January 1991), *Asian and Pacific Islander Population: March 1991 and 1990*; *Hispanic Population: March 1991*; and 1980 Census, *General Economic and Social Characteristics*.

[6]Technical, Sales and Administrative Support, and Precision Production, Craft and Repair occupations as a % of Total Employed Medium to Higher Skilled Nonprofessionals. Estimated from data in *Employment and Earnings* (January 1991); *Asian and Pacific Islander Population: March 1991 and 1990*; *Hispanic Population: March 1991*; and 1980 Census, *General Economic and Social Characteristics*.

[7]Services (except protective), Farm Workers and related occupations, and Operators, Fabricators and Laborers as a % of Total Employed Lower Skilled and Unskilled Workers. Estimated from data in *Employment and Earnings* (January 1991); *Asian and Pacific Islander Population: March 1991 and 1990*; *Hispanic Population: March 1991*; and 1980 Census, *General Economic and Social Characteristics*.

[8]Mean income for persons (15 years and over), in 1991 dollars. Sources: *Money Income of Households, 1989*, Table B-14; 1980 Census, *Detailed Population Characteristics*, Table 293.

[9]Median annual income of persons (15 years and over), in 1991 dollars. Value for Asians is estimated from data in *Asian and Pacific Islander Population: March 1991 and 1990*. Sources: *Money Income of Households, 1991*, Table B-14; 1980 Census, *General Economic and Social Characteristics*, Table 170.

[10]Calculated for the population over 25 years of age. Value for Hispanics in 1990 is for 1988. Estimated from data in: *Asian and Pacific Islander Population: March 1991 and 1990*; *Black Population: March 1991*; *Digest of Education Statistics: 1990 and 1987*; and 1980 Census, *General Economic and Social Characteristics*.

[11]Calculated for the population over 25 years of age completing 4 or more years of college. Value for Hispanics in 1990 is for 1988. Estimated from data in: *Asian and Pacific Islander Population: March 1991 and 1990*; *Black Population: March 1991*; *Digest of Education Statistics: 1990*; and 1980 Census, *General Economic and Social Characteristics*.

[12]All values for Whites and Blacks do not include Hispanics. Source: *Digest of Education Statistics: 1990*, Table 191. 1990 % is for 1988.

expectancy is lower for blacks than for whites and lower than the national average. Infant mortality is higher for Native Americans and blacks than for whites and higher than the national average. Blacks, Native Americans, Hispanics, and Asians have higher population growth rates than those of whites and national averages.

In Table 2-2, it appears that females exceed males in the total population among whites and blacks, but they receive less income than their proportionate size and a lower percentage of the income than their participation rate in the labor force. However, they suffer less from unemployment than males, probably because they have lower recorded participation rates in the labor force. White women have lower representation than white men among professionals, but black women have a higher representation among professionals than black men. However, Hispanic women and men are equally represented among professionals. Females are overrepresented relative to males among high school graduates of all groups. Apparently more males than females drop out of school. Finally, females are underrepresented among the lower skilled and underskilled of all groups. Whether this is due to underrecording is not clear.

RELEVANT ECONOMIC PRINCIPLES

1. National aggregate income data are indispensable in economic analysis. However, these aggregate data hide the distribution patterns, problem areas, and the segments of population that need attention most to achieve maximum output and efficiency. Therefore, incomes per capita and per family would be more useful from a policy standpoint if they were differentiated by ethnic, racial, gender group affiliation, given the wide variations between family sizes, dependency ratios, and income levels of these groups, and given that cultural or gender affiliation affects economic behavior.

Implications: National accounts need to be supplemented with details regarding constituent groups in the population. Policies dealing with unemployment, education, training, health, housing, and other infrastructures, as well as with poverty, would be much more effective if they were based on differentiated or disaggregated data.

2. If all people are economically rational in the sense that they want to maximize their income or utility as individuals, we should expect distributions among individual groups to be similar to those for the total population. However, major differences exist. Why? Are there different utility functions for different groups? Are their productivity levels different? Do they have different incentive systems? For example, are there joint family or group economic decisions, rather than individual rationalities to consider? Do cultural, ethnic, and racial variations affect the meaning of rationality? What constitutes utility for each group? For example, how do attitudes toward fertility and family size differ and how do they affect education, skills, and investment in human capital?

Implications: Economic policy that ignores these group differences may miss the target and thus help perpetuate the differences and the resulting waste. Taking such differences into consideration should be helpful in designing policy and increasing its effectiveness.

Suggestions for Students. Try to find out what differences in economic behavior among your friends and acquaintances may be related to racial, ethnic, or gender differences. What recommendations could follow from this informal field study regarding population, education, and employment policy making from your own standpoint?

3

GROUP DIVERSITY AND CONSUMER BEHAVIOR

It is generally agreed that consumption expenditure generates demand, regenerates human energy, prepares students, workers, and others for better performance, and enhances economic growth. Since consumption expenditure depends on purchasing power, and purchasing power depends largely on income, incomes that are inadequate to satisfy basic needs impair the quality of life and the performance of the population. Inadequate consumer expenditure also means lower aggregate demand, a lower expenditure multiplier, and a slowdown of the economy.

Given that the expenditure multiplier is directly related to the marginal propensity to consume ($k = (\frac{1}{1\text{-MPC}})$, the higher the percentage of every additional income dollar consumed, the higher will be the value of the multiplier, and the higher the impact of the added expenditure on aggregate income. Therefore, it should be more efficient to disaggregate the average marginal propensity to consume by income groups in order to identify groups that would spend more of their additional income on consumption as a way of promoting economic growth, as well as helping income groups that have more potential to raise their incomes by reducing their underutilization.

To illustrate, assume that the average MPC = 0.75; then the multiplier $k = (\frac{1}{1-0.75}) = (\frac{1}{0.25}) = 4$. Expenditure (investment) of \$100 will result in $\Delta Y = kI = 4 \times 100 = \$400$ additional income.

Suppose, however, that there are three separate group MPCs: 0.6, 0.75, and 0.9. Let the added investment expenditure of \$100 be reallocated so that \$50 is targeted toward generating income for group 1, \$20 toward group 2, and \$30 toward group 3. Then,

$$\Delta Y = k_1I_1 + k_2I_2 + k_3I_3 = \left(\frac{1}{1-0.6}\right) 50 + \left(\frac{1}{1-0.75}\right) 20 + \left(\frac{1}{1-0.9}\right) 30$$

$$= (2.5 \times 50) + (4 \times 20) + (10 \times 30)$$

$$= 125 + 80 + 300 = \underline{505}$$

Thus, targeting expenditure toward the higher MPC groups would be a more efficient investment expenditure policy.

It has been debated, however, whether race (or ethnic difference) is a major factor in explaining the difference in marginal propensities to consume between whites and blacks. For example, according to Sawyer, race by itself is not a factor in determining consumption patterns, although it may be one of many contributive factors.[3]

A similar conclusion was reached at by Stafford, Cox, and Higginbotham. They found differences in consumption patterns between blacks and whites with regard to expenditures on food, soft drinks, liquor, personal hygiene, and major appliances. However, most of the differences "were explainable more in terms of income or sociodemographic variations than by purely racial influences."[4]

On the other hand, the composition of the consumer basket has an impact on the demand function, whether it relies heavily on domestic production or on imports, whether it is seasonal or permanent, and whether it is primarily composed of basic or luxury items. This composition, however, may be directly influenced by racial, ethnic, or gender diversity and taste. Therefore, knowledge of the composition of consumer demand

and its relationship to the cultural background of the group, in addition to the level of income and size of the group should have major policy implications. The diversity of consumer behavior is illustrated in Table 3-1.

As Table 3-1 shows, Hispanics and blacks spend more of their incomes than do whites. However, blacks and Hispanics spend more and Asians spend less than whites on food as a percentage of income. Since Hispanics and blacks have lower per capita and family incomes than do whites and Asians, and spend higher percentages of their incomes on consumption, particularly on food, these minority groups may have higher marginal propensities to consume and less resources left for saving, risk taking, and other discretionary expenditures.

TABLE 3-1
EXPENDITURE BY HOUSEHOLDS HEADED
BY PERSONS 25-44 YEARS OLD, 1987[1]

	All Households	White[2] Households	Black[2] Households	Native American Households	Hispanic Households	Asian2 Households
% Expenditure of Income	98.2	90.5	96.4	NA	98.4	90.7
% Expenditure on Food	14.9	14.7	16.9	NA	18.4	14.2

[1]Based on data in Patricia Myers, *Family Economics Review*, 4, 2 (1991), Table 4. "All Households" is for all aged heads of household and is taken from *Consumer Expenditure Survey: 1987*, (Bulletin 2354), Table 7.

[2]Non-Hispanic (that is, Hispanics are not included).

NA: Not Available.

In Table 3-2, which compares consumption and total expenditures of blacks and whites at 4 points (years) in time, it appears that blacks spend a much higher percentage of their total expenditures on consumption than do whites. Another significant difference is the relatively high percentage spent by blacks on food, clothing, and personal care, compared with the much smaller percentage spent on education and health. It is also evident that either whites overspend on education and

TABLE 3-2
ANNUAL FAMILY CONSUMPTION EXPENDITURE, 1960-1990[1]

	1960		1972		1980		1985		1990	
	White	Black	White	Black	White	Black	White	Black	White	Black
Food[2]	1,474	1,104	1,867	1,534	3,738	2,867	4,158	2,778	5,028	3,507
Clothing	534	446	645	665	916	736	1,443	1,235	1,642	1,407
Housing	1,554	1,114	2,621	1,924	5,067	3,614	7,327	5,099	9,212	6,345
Transportation	820	458	1,646	1,192	3,548	2,401	4,786	2,914	5,370	3,210
Entertainment[3]	262	159	805	329	886	462	1,387	673	1,687	706
Education	57	28	111	56	218	142	331	244	432	208
Health Care	362	182	557	288	774	392	1,166	630	1,570	780
Personal Care	150	133	170	123	156	128	307	267	372	301
Miscellaneous[4]	120	61	89	48	271	162	546	387	676	408
Current Consumption:	5,333	3,685	8,510	6,158	15,574	10,904	21,451	14,227	25,989	16,872
Personal Insurance	318	205	758	516	1,243	911	2,098	1,326	2,705	1,721
Gifts and Contributions	301	149	539	236	518	201	850	426	852	538
Total Expenditures:	5,952	4,039	9,807	6,910	17,335	12,016	24,399	15,979	29,546	19,131
Income after taxes:	NA	NA	10,078	6,743	17,252	12,174	23,690	16,062	29,955	20,908
Savings	-	-	271	-167	-83	158	-709	83	409	1,777

[1]Expressed in current dollars. Values for 1960 are for "Whites" and "Nonwhites" in 1960-1961; for 1972 are for "Whites" and "Blacks" in 1972-1973; for 1980-1990 are for "Whites and Others" and "Blacks." 1990 Income after taxes is estimated from *U.S. Department of Labor News Release: 91-607* (November 22, 1991), Table 7. *Consumer Expenditure Survey: 1984-1986* (Bulletin 2333), Table 17. *1980-1981* (Bulletin 2225). Table 24, and *1972-1973* (Bulletin 1992), Table 4; *Expenditure Patterns of the American Family.*

[2]Includes alcohol and tobacco.

[3]Includes recreation, reading materials, etc.

[4]Includes legal expenses, funeral expenses, etc.

NA: Not Available.

health, which is unlikely, or that blacks underspend, which is more likely. In other words, blacks are not receiving adequate endowment in the form of education and basic health care. Whether it is a cultural phenomenon that blacks spend relatively more on clothing than on education, or a function of their relatively low incomes and the necessity of spending more on clothing as a basic need, which is the likely explanation, will make a difference in policy making. Blacks were savers in three of the four years surveyed and whites were savers in only two, which tends to contradict the data in Table 3-1. Through the 1980s, white family savings were on the average about 84% of black family savings, measured as income minus consumption expenditure.

These conclusions are still subject to evaluation. Various studies have reached different results, as shown in Table 3-3, which summarizes findings of different scholars.

As concluded by Alexis:

1. Total consumption expenditures of Negroes are less than for comparable income whites, or, Negroes save more out of a given income than do whites with the same incomes.

2. Negro consumers spend more for clothing and non-automobile transportation and less for food, housing, medical care and automobile transportation than do comparable income whites.

3. There is no consistent racial difference in expenditures for either recreation and leisure or home furnishing and equipment at comparable income levels.[5]

RELEVANT ECONOMIC PRINCIPLES

1. Engels' Law says that the percentage of family income spent on food tends to decline as family income rises.

Do the levels of expenditures on food vary only according to levels of income, or do they also vary according to ethnic or gender groupings? Are there income thresholds to be reached

TABLE 3-3
SUMMARY STATEMENT OF FINDINGS FOR STUDIES OF WHETHER NEGROES SPEND MORE OR LESS THAN COMPARABLE WHITES

Study	Food	Housing	Clothing	Recreation and Leisure	Home Furnishings and Equipment	Medical Care	Auto Transportation	Non-Auto Transportation
Edwards	less	less	more	more	less	-	-	-
Sterner	less	more*	more	less	less	less	-	-
B. L. S. Detroit	less	less	more	more	more	less	less	more
B. L. S. Houston	less	less	less	more	less	less	less	more
B. L. S. Washington	more	more	more	less	less	less	less	more
B. L. S. Memphis	less	less	more	less	mixed	less	less	more
Friend and Kravis	less	less	more	less	more	less	less	more
Fact Finders	less	-	-	-	-	-	-	-

*In the southern villages there was no difference.

Edwards and Sterner discuss transportation, but do not make a breakdown by auto and non-auto.

Source: Marcus Alexis, "Some Negro-White Differences in Consumption," in Joyce and Govoni, op. cit, p. 272. *Some data and additional details may be found in Marcus Alexis, George H. Haines, and Leonard S. Simon, *Black Consumer Profiles and Food Purchasing in the Inner City*, University of Michigan, 1980.

before the percentage of expenditure on food begins to decline? For example, rising incomes in developing countries have tended to be accompanied by relatively higher expenditures on consumer goods, including food, up to a certain level of income before the percentage of such expenditure begins to decline. This threshold level may also vary according to cultural differences.

Implications: Knowing these differences would dictate differentiated economic policies, depending on the expected impact of these policies on consumption, saving, demand, and supply.

2. An Inferior Good is a commodity for which the demand goes down as incomes go up. It is possible that inferior goods are consumed more by lower-income groups than by others, and more by certain ethnic and gender groups than by others. Inferior goods for one group may be normal goods for others.

Implications: Identifying consumers of inferior goods would help refine economic policy and increase its efficiency. It would also help the business community to forecast market demand for those goods.

3. A Giffen Good is a commodity whose demand increases as its price increases, whether for snobbish reasons, conspicuous consumption, or stereotypical beliefs that higher prices mean better quality. Certain brands of cars sell more because of their high price than because their quality is higher than that of other brands. To what extent are such goods consumed more by certain income or ethnic groups than by others? To what extent does such expenditure compensate for other deprivations or feelings of inferiority? How does such expenditure affect spending on other goods or services, for example, education?

Implications: Identifying the groups that consume the Giffen Good and the motivations for their behavior would help refine economic and business policy, target it more accurately, and thus increase its efficiency.

In all of the cases above, knowledge of the details could improve accuracy in targeting segments of the market, make better use of the multiplier concept, improve forecasting, and influence stability of the market.

Suggestions for Students. Identify as many Inferior and Giffen goods as you can and the groups most attracted to them. Any policy recommendations?

4

SAVING AND INVESTMENT

Saving and investing behaviors are two different roles, sometimes performed by the same people; more frequently, savers
and investors are different people, and the decisions to save
(not consume) and to invest are only indirectly related.

Saving is usually associated with the level of income, and
investment with the expected returns, on the assumption that
people behave in accordance with economic rationality, choice,
and a given priority system. However, these decisions are
rarely associated with cultural or gender affiliation. Yet, as has
been noted, certain ethnic groups are likely to have higher marginal propensities to save and invest than others. It is also likely that consumption and saving marginal propensities do not
add up to one. Certain groups may consume little and hoard
their unspent incomes. Still others may invest in less productive activities than others to avoid risk or because of tradition,
culture, or prejudice. While knowledge of national behavior
patterns may be sufficient for overall policy planning, evaluation, and prediction, it is not sufficient to direct or influence
policy. Knowledge of behavior details could be of strategic
importance in dealing with economic fluctuations, regional and
sectoral development, and policy implementation.

Though saving behavior is usually explained as a reflection
of consumption decisions since what is not consumed is being

saved, it is difficult to separate decisions to consume from decisions to save, especially if one were to explain consumption-saving behavior. In his summary of major studies of saving behavior among whites and blacks, Marcus Alexis notes the following:[6]

1. "Negroes had smaller deficits or larger surpluses than comparable income whites and. . . the break-even income for Negroes was fifty percent of what it was for whites." [Mendershausen]

2. "At comparable incomes Negroes save more than whites." [Brady and Friedman and Duesenberry]

3. Such behavioral differences may be explained by differences in asset holding and access to credit. Those who have more assets and easier access to credit tend to spend more and save less, or even dissave more than those with less assets and more limited access to credit. [Tobin]

4. Saving (expenditure) behavior varies according to localities, North or South. Southern blacks save less than Southern whites or Northern blacks with similar incomes. One explanation may be that Southern blacks do not use conventional or institutional saving methods and hence the findings are underestimates. Another is that upper-income blacks spend more or save less than whites with comparable incomes because of their social responsibility, but much less than whites who are community leaders with much higher incomes. [Klein and Mooney]

5. General explanatory variables include: Liquid assets, disposable income, race, and job security.

6. Finally, economic variables alone do not explain the consumption-saving differences between blacks and whites. Other factors must be taken into consideration. [Klein and Mooney]

TABLE 4-1
PERCENT OF HOUSEHOLDS OWNING VARIOUS
INTEREST-EARNING ASSETS, BY RACE, 1984, 1988[1]

	1984				1988			
	White	Black	Hispanic[2]	Other[3]	White	Black	Hispanic[2]	Other[3]
Held at Financial Institutions:								
Passbook Savings	65.7	41.6	46.9	58.6	64.2	40.7	45.6	63.2
Money Market Deposit	17.4	2.6	5.0	13.9	16.7	3.4	5.0	16.1
Certificates of Deposit	21.2	4.2	6.3	10.6	19.6	4.3	6.5	13.6
Interest-earning Checking	27.0	7.2	11.9	30.1	37.0	13.0	17.4	37.8
Total[4]	75.4	43.8	50.8	69.2	76.6	44.5	51.0	72.4
Other Interest-earning Assets:								
Money Market Funds	4.2	0.9	1.1	2.5	4.0	0.5	1.0	3.3
U.S. Government Securities	1.6	0.1	0.1	0	2.5	0.1	0.2	0.7
Muni & Corp. Bonds[5]	2.9	0.3	0.1	2.2	3.1	0.3	0.4	0.7
Other Assets[6]	3.0	1.0	0.8	3.9	3.6	1.6	0.9	1.6
Total	9.4	2.1	2.0	4.9	10.5	1.9	2.4	5.2

[1]Sources: *Household Wealth and Asset Ownership: 1988*, Table 4, and *1984*, Table 2.

[2]Hispanics may be of any race.

[3]Other races includes Asians and Native Americans. Values estimated from data provided in sources above. Over 75% of "Other" are Asians.

[4]All interest-earning assets held at financial institutions.

[5]Municipal and corporate bonds.

[6]All other interest-earning assets.

Fiscal policy, for example, would be more effective if changes in government expenditures and tax rates were related to the size of the income groups whose economic rationalities are influenced more by culture and tradition than by material gain or by government fiscal policy. For example, will a higher marginal tax rate reduce incentives or will it increase incentives because it forces people to work harder to cope with certain expectations or obligations, such as being able to pay the rent on a home or on a farm?

TABLE 4-2
PERCENT OF HOUSEHOLDS OWNING VARIOUS
INTEREST-EARNING ASSET TYPES, BY RACE, 1984, 1988[1]

	1984				1988			
	White	Black	Hispanic[2]	Other[3]	White	Black	Hispanic[2]	Other[3]
Interest-earning Assets at Financial Institutions[4]	75.4	43.8	50.8	69.2	76.6	44.5	51.0	72.4
Other Interest-earning Assets[5]	9.4	2.1	2.0	4.9	10.5	1.9	2.4	5.2
Checking Accounts	56.9	32.0	36.6	44.7	50.9	30.1	34.4	39.0
Stocks and Mutual Funds	22.0	5.4	7.5	13.8	23.9	7.0	7.6	15.8
Own Business	14.0	4.0	9.6	13.8	13.6	3.7	8.5	15.0
Motor Vehicles	88.5	65.0	74.6	82.9	89.2	64.7	73.7	83.4
Own Home	67.3	43.8	39.9	48.2	66.7	43.5	42.7	46.4
Rental Property	10.1	6.6	6.6	13.8	9.6	4.6	6.5	9.5
Other Real Estate	10.9	3.3	5.8	7.9	11.4	4.4	7.1	6.7
Mortgages	3.3	0.1	1.1	1.1	2.5	0.4	1.0	1.4
U.S. Savings Bonds	16.1	7.4	6.1	9.6	18.5	11.0	9.5	13.6
IRA/KEOGH Accounts	21.4	5.1	9.1	16.3	26.4	6.9	10.7	24.1
Other Assets[6]	3.9	0.7	1.1	1.7	3.6	0.8	1.4	3.1

[1]Sources: *Household Wealth and Asset Ownership: 1988*, Table 3, and *1984*, Table 1.

[2]Hispanics may be of any race.

[3]Other races includes Asians and Native Americans. Values estimated from data provided in sources above.

[4]All interest-earning assets at financial institutions; includes passbook accounts, money market deposit accounts, certificates of deposit, and interest-earning checking accounts.

[5]Other interest-earning assets; includes money market funds, U.S. government securities, municipal and corporate bonds, and other interest-earning assets.

[6] Includes unit trusts and other financial investments.

Monetary policy would also be greatly affected by the failure of certain income groups to deposit their savings in financial institutions, their slow or limited response to changes in interest rates, and their limited participation in the money economy. To what extent are such behaviors associated with cultural and gender differences? A look at Tables 4-1 and 4-2 should help.

Major differences between ethnic groups in participation in the monetary economies are evident in every entry of Table 4-1. Blacks, Hispanics, and Other use savings accounts, money markets, certificates of deposit (CDs) and other money instruments less frequently than whites. The differences were evident in the use of CDs, money markets, and municipal and corporate bonds, even though some of these carry less risk than passbook saving accounts, which are more popular with all groups. Apparently, liquidity is important in all cases.

Similar differences are evident in asset ownership by households. For example, much smaller percentages of blacks and Hispanics than whites own stocks, businesses, homes, mortgages, and pension accounts. Though ownerships rose for all groups between 1984 and 1988, the group differences remained. These figures, however, indicate the percentages of owners in each group, but tell little about the value of the assets held by each group. It is safe to assume that blacks and Hispanics own less than their proportionate size in the population.

Table 4-3 shows the variation in asset value by ethnic origin of asset holders. It appears that the median values of the asset holdings of blacks and Hispanics in 1984 were below those of whites, and with minor exceptions the same applied in 1988. Therefore, not only do whites have more holdings of each asset type, but the average values of whites' holdings are greater than those of blacks and Hispanics. However, when blacks are compared with Hispanics, it appears that the median asset values of Hispanics are higher than those of blacks.

The question arises whether the smaller percentage of blacks and Hispanics among asset holders is due to their fewer resources and lower incomes or to their cultural and traditional behaviors. Most probably both factors are important. Lower-income whites would no doubt have a smaller share in these markets than more affluent whites. But it is apparent that the average share of the minorities is smaller than the average

TABLE 4-3
MEDIAN VALUE OF HOLDINGS FOR ASSET OWNERS, BY RACIAL/ETHNIC GROUP, 1984, 1988[1]

	1984			1988		
	White	Black	Hispanic[2]	White	Black	Hispanic[2]
Interest-earning Assets at Financial Institutions[3]	3,457	739	1,178	4,024	939	1,521
Other Interest-earning Assets[4]	9,826	(-)[5]	(-)[5]	11,199	3,218	7,217
Checking Accounts	457	318	359	490	428	411
Stocks and Mutual Funds	3,908	2,777	2,488	4,931	2,259	2,920
Equity in Own Business	7,113	2,054	6,580	10,751	1,033	4,784
Equity in Own Motor Vehicles	4,293	2,691	3,091	4,593	5,868	3,341
Equity in Own Home	41,999	24,077	38,867	44,546	26,683	38,478
Equity in Rental Property	34,516	27,291	23,772	38,052	28,658	34,121
Equity in Other Real Estate	15,488	10,423	10,689	18,510	10,647	10,910
U.S. Savings Bonds	305	200	258	583	325	379
IRA/KEOGH Accounts	4,922	2,450	3,257	9,287	4,129	5,318
Other Assets[6]	13,089	(-)[5]	(-)[5]	16,271	17,738	9,345
Net Worth	39,135	3,397	4,913	43,279	4,169	5,524

[1]In current dollars. Sources: *Household Wealth and Asset Ownership: 1988*, Table 2, and *1984*, Table 2.

[2]Hispanics may be of any race.

[3]Includes passbook accounts, money market deposit accounts, certificates of deposit, and interest-earning checking accounts.

[4]Includes money market funds, U.S. government securities, municipal and corporate bonds, and other interest-earning assets.

[5]Unable to report because of insufficient sample size.

[6]Includes unit trusts and other financial investments.

share of the majority. Whether whites, blacks, and Hispanics earning similar incomes would have similar behavioral patterns in the money economy is not clear.[7] Our hypothesis is that there would be differences and that whites would be more active participants, higher risk takers than their black and

Hispanic counterparts, and owners of a larger share of the assets than their proportionate size in the population.

RELEVANT ECONOMIC PRINCIPLES

1. Fiscal policy is based on the assumption that all agents in the market are responsive to changes in the economy, including fiscal policy, and that resource mobility spreads the effects through a trickle-down mechanism so that all segments of the population are affected.

However, since ethnic groups vary in the degree of their participation in business ownership and direct and portfolio investment, the impact of fiscal and monetary policy is bound to benefit the active participants more than others. Government expenditure and changes in the marginal tax rate may be expected to benefit those who own businesses, especially those related to government contracts, and those whose income is high enough to be affected by changes in their marginal tax rates. Those who do not own a business and lower-income groups would be affected only indirectly by a national fiscal policy. Fiscal policy would be much more effective if such differences between income and ethnic groups were taken into consideration in formulating and implementing policy. Conversely, to design fiscal policy on the basis of averages for the total population of consumers would undermine the effectiveness of such policy in dealing with common economic problems.

Furthermore, both data collection and policy analysis would be enhanced by applying differentiated policies according to behavioral patterns of the culturally diverse groups in the population.

2. Monetary policy is based on the assumption that most people are active in the money economy and that they respond to changes in interest rates and rates of return. Inactivity in the money economy and failure to respond to policy changes indicate market imperfection and they undermine policy effective-

ness. Therefore, if certain ethnic groups are more active in the money economy than others, and the differences in activity may be traced to cultural, ethnic, racial, and gender differences, monetary policy would be influenced by recognizing these differences.

Implications: To overcome market imperfection, monetary policy would be more influential if it were differentiated, that is, targeted both toward the groups that respond readily to changes, and toward those that do not, in order to engage them in the economy. National policy is adequate to elicit responses by the first group, but to influence the behavior of the less responsive groups, modifications of or alternatives to standard monetary policy may be necessary. For example, policies could be modified to include lower-interest loans, easier credits, education in the use of banking services, special insurance programs for new businesses, and other subsidies to the groups and locations that need help in consistency with the objectives of monetary policy.

To illustrate multiple fiscal policies with some emphasis on targeted areas, it is possible to construct programs that focus on rehabilitation of the infrastructure in areas in which the targeted groups reside. That would both elevate their living standards and provide them with jobs. Such programs would be in addition to national fiscal policy programs, though expenditures on the latter might have to be reduced. Another type of fiscal policy may be one that provides tax credits, tax exemption, or direct subsidies to businesses in the targeted areas, or owned by the targeted groups. Still another approach would be to establish a public contracting office to offer government contracts to bidders from the targeted groups. In all these cases, there is good reason to expect the specific fiscal policy to be at least as effective as the national policy and to have the added benefit of rescuing economically depressed areas and population groups.

One version of monetary policy that might directly benefit targeted groups would be the establishment of a credit system that includes a program to educate those groups in the use of loans and to extend loans to them for productive uses at easier terms than the competitive market for a given period of time. Such an approach might be especially useful in the construction industry and in making home ownership available. Another approach would be to make it easier for small financial institutions run by the targeted groups to participate in financing the government deficit.

Suggestions for Students: Find out how members of various racial, ethnic, and gender groups behave in regard to borrowing, purchasing government bonds, and playing the stock market. Make recommendations to increase participation of those who do not participate much in the market economy, if you think their participation is desirable.

5

POVERTY, THE UNDERCLASS, AND ECONOMIC POLICY

Poverty in economic terms may be defined as having to live on an income below the minimum necessary to satisfy basic needs as institutionally specified. Such an income indicates the poverty line, which changes with changes in the economy and society. We may assume that the poverty line income is not higher than the income earned for full-time work by the least skilled person in the labor force.

An underclass, as it has become known, includes those who are living in chronic or "institutionalized" poverty; some members of the underclass may be working full time but earning less than the poverty line income.

Both concepts imply that certain members of the labor force are unable to earn the minimum income, either because of their own behavior, such as choosing not to work diligently or full-time, or because of the socioeconomic or political environment in which they live, as in situations of chronic unemployment. If their incomes while working are below the poverty line, we may assume that their levels of productivity are below their potential. If so, their poverty and underclass status represent underutilization, a loss to the economy equal to the additional output they would have produced, or the income they would have earned, had they been able to produce at their potential. If so, those in poverty and the underclass must face obstacles that

TABLE 5-1
FAMILIES BELOW THE POVERTY LINE, BY
RACE/ETHNIC GROUP AND TYPE OF FAMILY, 1970-1990[1]

	1970	1975	1980	1985	1990
All Families:					
White[2]	8.0	7.7	8.0	9.1	8.1
Black[2]	29.5	27.1	28.9	28.7	29.3
Hispanic	NA	25.1	23.2	25.5	25.0
Mexican	NA	NA	21.6	24.4	25.0
Puerto Rican	NA	NA	40.4	40.6	37.5
Other Races[3]	11.9	12.6	15.3	15.6	13.8
Families by Type:[4]					
Single Parent	NA	40.8	40.1	41.4	40.5
Female Head	43.8	44.0	42.9	45.4	44.5
Nonwhite Female Head	NA	57.2	55.1	57.9	55.2

[1]Sources: *Poverty in the United States: 1991*, Table 32; *The Hispanic Population in the United States: 1991*, Table 4; *The Asian and Pacific Islander Population in the United States: March 1991 and 1990*, Table 8; *Poverty in the United States: 1987*, Table 32, and *1985*, Table 32; *Characteristics of the Population Below the Poverty Level: 1980*, Table 39.

[2]May include Hispanics.

[3]Primarily Asian and Pacific Islanders; also includes Native Americans. (Note: In 1990, the rate for Asian and Pacific Islanders is 11.0%.)

[4]With children under 18 years old. Female Head implies no husband present. Single Parent and Nonwhite Female Head are calculated from data provided in the sources above.

NA: Not Available.

make it impossible for them to perform at a minimum or at the level of the least skilled person. The question then is: Why? Is it because of personal circumstances or general economic conditions? In either case one may ask: how can economic policy help solve the problem of poverty and the underclass? First, let us find out who are the poor and the underclass.

TABLE 5-2
MEDIAN WAGES FOR FULL-TIME WORKERS, 1970-1990[1]

	1970	1975	1980	1985	1990
(Total) Males	389	411	379	377	371
(Total) Females	242	255	244	257	266
White Males[2]	405	418	399	388	380
White Females[2]	245	257	250	261	272
Black Males[2]	291	322	300	283	275
Black Females[2]	209	242	231	234	236
Hispanic Males	NA	NA	289	274	246
Hispanic Females	NA	NA	215	213	214

[1]Median weekly wages in constant dollars, deflated by CPI-U (1982-1984 = 100). Calculated from data in: *Employment and Earnings*, January 1992, Table 54; *Handbook of Labor Statistics* (Bulletin 2340), Table 41; *Statistical Abstract of the United States, 1981*, Table 681.

[2]May include Hispanics.

NA: Not Available.

Table 5-1 shows that all racial and ethnic groups, including whites, have a share in poverty. However, black and Hispanic families suffer most; about a quarter of all such families have been living in poverty, as officially defined, for the last two decades. Whites and Native Americans also suffer poverty to a significant degree. Up to 9% of all white families and more than 15% of Other families, mostly Native Americans and Asians, live in poverty. Table 5-2 shows that females, even those who are fully employed, are more vulnerable to the threats of poverty than males among all racial and ethnic groups. Families headed by females, by unskilled workers, and by single parents, male or female, are the most vulnerable to poverty. Though the size of the underclass is not estimated, the persistent high rate of poverty suggests that a significant percentage of the poor in recent years could qualify as underclass. The latest figures indicate that 13.4% of American families are classified as poor.

Another indicator of male-female inequality of earnings is shown in Table 5-3. An interesting pattern is illustrated by these figures. Females exceed male percentages in the income brackets ranging from under $2,500 to $17,499. In all brackets above that range, male percentages exceed those of females. Could this be due solely to the different rates of participation of the two groups?

Table 5-4 shows the distribution of net worth by racial-ethnic affiliation for 1984 and 1988. The pattern is the same as suggested above. All groups have households with zero or negative net worth, though blacks and Hispanics exceed all others in this category. In contrast, blacks and Hispanics are

TABLE 5-3
INCOME DISTRIBUTION BY SEX, 1991[1]

	Persons by Sex			Persons by Sex	
	Males	Females		Males	Females
Number (thousand)	88,653	92,569	$22,500 to $24,999	3.9	3.4
Total (%)	100.0	100.0	$25,000 to $29,999	8.4	5.7
Under $2,500	6.6	14.8	$30,000 to $34,999	7.2	3.9
$2,500 to $4,999	5.5	11.7	$35,000 to $39,999	5.8	2.7
$5,000 to $7,499	6.8	12.7	$40,000 to $44,999	4.7	1.7
$7,500 to $9,999	6.2	9.0	$45,000 to $49,999	3.3	1.1
$10,000 to $12,499	7.2	8.9	$50,000 to $54,999	2.9	0.7
$12,500 to $14,499	5.4	6.1	$55,000 to $64,999	2.9	0.7
$15,000 to $17,499	6.2	6.3	$65,000 to $74,499	1.7	0.4
$17,500 to $19,999	5.0	4.6	$75,000 to $99,999	2.3	0.4
$20,000 to $22,499	6.0	5.0	$100,000 and over	2.0	0.3

[1]Persons, with income, 15 years old and over on March 1992. Totals may not sum to 100% because of rounding.

Source: *Money Income of Households, Families, and Persons in the United States: 1991,* Table 26.

the smallest percentages among those in the high net worth brackets. While almost 30% of whites have a net worth of $100,000 or more, only about 6% of blacks and 12% of Hispanics are in that bracket.

RELEVANT ECONOMIC PRINCIPLES

1. Economists are fond of arguing that one makes a choice between work and leisure. However, to what extent does a person who lacks the means to satisfy basic needs have a choice?

TABLE 5-4
DISTRIBUTION OF HOUSEHOLD
NET WORTH, BY RACE, 1984, 1988[1]

	1984				1988			
	White	Black	Hispanic[2]	Other[3]	White	Black	Hispanic[2]	Other[3]
Zero or Negative	8.4	30.5	23.9	16.4	8.7	29.1	23.8	11.8
$1 to $4,999	14.0	23.9	26.3	23.6	13.9	22.8	24.8	23.0
$5,000 to $9,999	6.3	6.8	7.6	8.3	5.9	8.1	6.5	7.1
$10,000 to $24,999	12.2	14.0	11.4	12.3	11.5	11.6	11.2	11.6
$25,000 to $49,999	15.0	11.7	9.5	8.8	13.1	12.9	10.7	10.9
$50,000 to $99,999	20.7	9.3	13.1	14.0	17.7	10.3	11.3	11.8
$100,000 to $249,000	16.9	3.3	5.1	12.0	19.3	4.4	9.3	15.1
$250,000 to $499,999	4.4	0.5	2.1	5.6	6.7	0.7	1.9	6.5
$500,000 or over	2.1	0.1	1.0	2.9	3.2	0.1	0.5	1.9
Median (in 1988 dollars)	$44,396	$3,807	$5,548	$13,492	$43,279	$4,169	$5,524	$17,913

[1]Sources: *Household Wealth and Asset Ownership: 1988*, Table 5, and *1984*, Table 4.

[2]Hispanics may be of any race.

[3]Primarily Asian and Pacific Islanders and Native Americans (the former compose 72% of this group). Values estimated from data provided in sources above.

[4]Median Household Net Worth in terms of 1988 dollars. Values for "Other" were estimated using two methods of interpolation (both linear and Pareto); then the lower estimate was reported above (the higher estimates, in 1988 dollars, for 1984 and 1988 were $14,388 and $19,929 respectively).

Is it other than choosing between living and dying? Does a backward-bending labor supply curve actually exist? In the absence of choice, the market mechanism breaks down, at least with regard to those having no choice. In that case, there is little reason to expect them to be able to overcome their economic crises within the framework of the market economy. Then their poverty tends to become chronic and they tend to join the ranks of the underclass.

Implications: Before choice can be exercised, one must be able to satisfy basic needs, which the poor are not able to do, especially among women and segregated minorities. For the poor and disadvantaged to be able to satisfy basic needs and to exercise choice, some controlled intervention in the market may be indispensable.

2. Poverty and the underclass are economic burdens to the economy as well as to individuals, regardless of race, ethnicity, or gender. The causes of poverty and the underclass, however, may be related to a group's racial, ethnic, or gender affiliation.

Implications: Treating poverty and the underclass is a social responsibility as much as it is an individual responsibility, because poverty and the underclass imply waste and a loss to the economy, regardless of who the poor and underclass happen to be.

3. Low incomes are normal in any given pattern of distribution of income. Living in poverty, as defined above, however, is not normal for working people. Hence, existing poverty must be due to circumstances beyond the control of individuals, especially those who are fully employed. On the other hand, one must find out why certain people are not working, even though they want to work.

Implications: Economic policy would be most effective if it concentrated on raising above the poverty line the incomes of those working and on providing work for those unable to find it. For all others, a guarantee of a minimum income until they are able to work is the only way to overcome poverty and the underclass problem.

4. Work incentives are tied to the expected utility of the reward or the compensation for work. Those working below capacity may be doing so only because their expected compensation is lower than the utility of their not working up to capacity.

Work incentives may vary, depending on the individual's utility function, which may be influenced by cultural diversity. If people are aware of their own objectives, have a choice whether or not to work for those objectives, and are fairly certain that working for the objectives will help to realize them, they probably will not stay out of work voluntarily. If they do, they must have other reasons for doing so.

Implications: People who are "apparently" voluntarily unemployed, including those in the underclass, or in the group of "discouraged" workers, most likely cannot find jobs on their own, or they have lost hope of realizing their objectives through work. Economic policy would be more effective if their awareness of job availability were increased and their incentives revived. Furthermore, economic policy would be more effective if it recognized that certain cultural and traditional values indirectly generate incentives other than the material incentives usually glorified in the market economy. Identifying those incentives would help in designing more feasible and workable solutions to economic hardships faced by specific racial and ethnic groups.

5. Realized benefits may vary in composition, whether material or other, but will serve the same incentive function as long as they are based on free choice. The freedom to exercise choice of objectives which create incentives varies by ethnic or gender composition of the population.

Implications: Unless free choice of economic objectives is guaranteed for the various cultural and gender groups, their economic achievement will most likely be below potential.

Suggestions to Students: Identify direct and indirect nonmaterial incentives for economic activity that may be associated with cultural diversity. Interviewing other students or members of the community may be one way to do this.

Identify incentives offered by public programs to overcome poverty and the underclass status. See how much you can improve on these programs.

ECONOMIC DISCRIMINATION:
BENEFITS AND COSTS

Economic discrimination means that certain individuals or groups are treated differentially because of characteristics that are not directly related to their economic performance. In other words, certain members of society may receive unequal rewards for equal performance. Or they may enjoy fewer economic opportunities than others for reasons other than their potential performance, as in the case of discrimination because of racial, ethnic, or gender differences. Such discrimination is based on prejudice.

Economic discrimination because of prejudice has been common in the history of the United States and other societies. It continues to be a source of social cost to society and of deprivation for its victims. Those favored by discrimination receive benefits at the expense of society and of the victims of discrimination. Evidence of discrimination against racial, ethnic, and gender groups may be observed in incomes received, net worth, occupational structure, rates of employment and unemployment, and limited economic opportunities long before members of these groups enter the labor market. Tables 6-1, 6-2, and 6-3 provide illustrative data.

The data are abundantly clear: median incomes are differentiated by race, ethnicity, and sex. Blacks receive lower incomes

TABLE 6-1
MEDIAN REAL INCOME FOR PERSONS, 1960-1980[1]

	1960	1970	1980
White Males[2]	14,591	20,296	15,812
White Females[2]	4,868	9,634	6,527
Black Males[2]	7,615	13,387	9,509
Black Females[2]	3,378	7,753	5,675
Mexican Males	NA	12,204	10,750
Mexican Females	NA	4,876	5,529
Puerto Rican Males	9,916	13,289	10,339
Puerto Rican Females	6,483	7,469	5,428
Cuban Males	NA	14,258	12,438
Cuban Females	NA	7,281	6,441
Native American Males[3]	6,054	9,044	9,841
Native American Females[3]	3,378	4,374	5,180
Japanese Males	14,541	19,521	18,235
Japanese Females	6,645	8,340	8,993
Chinese Males	11,726	13,461	13,103
Chinese Females	6,983	6,923	7,359
Filipino Males	10,314	12,936	13,045
Filipino Females	5,128	9,054	10,016

Source: Based on data from Census of the Population – *General Economic and Social Characteristics*, Tables 164 and 170; 1970 Census, Tables 94, 97, and 121; *Subject Reports: Persons of Spanish Origin*, Table 7; *Subject Reports: American Indians*, Table 6; *Subject Reports: Japanese, Chinese and Filipinos in the United States*, Tables 6, 21, and 36; 1960 Census, *General Characteristics*, Table 97; *Subject Reports*: 1B, Table 6; 1C, Tables 32-36; 1D, Table 5.

[1]Deflated by CPI-U (1982-1984 = 100); dollar value averaged for 1982-1984 as a base value.

[2]May include Hispanics (except 1980).

[3] Does not include Eskimos or Aleuts.

NA: Not Available.

TABLE 6-2
REAL INCOME PER CAPITA, 1970-1990[1]

	1970	1975	1980	1985	1990
(Total) Males	24,087	24,037	23,084	23,800	19,925
(Total) Females	10,029	10,402	10,191	11,724	10,645
White Males[2]	25,056	24,966	24,028	24,803	20,767
White Females[2]	10,179	10,487	10,259	11,889	10,818
Black Males[2]	14,966	15,288	14,812	15,415	12,996
Black Females[2]	8,766	9,528	9,521	10,373	9,219
Hispanic Males	NA	17,701	17,303	16,699	13,353
Hispanic Females	NA	10,539	9,424	8,447	8,101

Source: Based on data from: *Money Income of Households, Families, and Persons in the United States: 1991*, Table B-14; *Money Income and Poverty Status in the United States: 1989*, Tables 13 and 17. Dollar value averaged for 1982-1984 as a base year.

[1]Deflated by CPI-U (1982-1984 = 100).

[2]May include Hispanics.

NA: Not Available.

than whites and Hispanics. Females receive lower incomes than males among all racial and ethnic groups. Table 6-2 shows the differential per capita real incomes received by males and females; females consistently receive lower real incomes than males. Home ownership is also unequally distributed among ethnic and racial groups, both in numbers and values. In all cases minorities fare with lower benefits than their proportional size in the population.

Some may argue that incomes are differentiated because performances are differentiated. If so, why are performances so widely differentiated? Most probably they are differentiated because of unequal opportunities for persons of equal qualifications. However, opportunities probably become unequal long before the individual enters the market and faces the challenge to perform. Hence, performance by definition had to be

TABLE 6-3
PERCENT OF OWNER-OCCUPIED HOUSING UNITS
AND MEDIAN VALUE: 1970, 1980, 1987[1]

	1970		1980		1987	
	% of units	Value	% of units	Value	% of units	Value
White	65.0	17,1004[4]	67.8	48,600	67.4	69,282
Black	41.6	10,600	44.4	27,200	43.5	48,786
Hispanic[2]	43.8	14,900	43.4	44,700	40.4	70,182
Native American[3]	50.0	13,500	53.2	34,400	46.0	54,073
Asian/Pacific Islander	NA	NA	52.4	83,112	46.0	136,843
Japanese	56.0	28,300	59.0	93,100	NA	NA
Chinese	44.1	29,300	54.5	89,600	NA	NA
Filipino	39.3	22,200	55.9	79,400	NA	NA
Korean	43.4	29,800	44.5	86,100	NA	NA
Indian	NA	NA	50.7	74,300	NA	NA
Vietnamese	NA	NA	26.7	56,800	NA	NA

Sources: *Housing Characteristics of Selected Races and Hispanic Origin Households in the US: 1987*, Tables 1, 4 and 7; 1980 Census of Housing, *General Housing Characteristics*, Tables 6-9; and 1970, *Subject Reports: Housing of Selected Racial Groups*, Tables A-1, and A-3; *Subject Reports: Housing Characteristics by Household Composition*, Tables A-1, A-6 and A-11; *Subject Reports: Structural Characteristics of the Housing Inventory*, Tables A-16 and A-29.

[1]Percent of owner-occupied housing units within each group. Values are expressed in current dollars and represent the median value of specified owner-occupied housing units per group. 1970 median values reflect median value of urban owner-occupied housing units (except for blacks and Hispanics).

[2]Hispanics may be of any race.

[3]1970 and 1980 values do not include Eskimos or Aleuts.

[4]Median value of owner-occupied housing for "all races." (Note: "Whites" own 94% of all owner-occupied housing).

NA: Not Available.

unequal. Though economic policy may not be equipped to look for causes of discrimination, it may be able to overcome some of the obstacles to improved performance.

However, studies have shown that even when comparisons show equality of performance, the distribution of rewards tends to be biased against minorities and females because of discrimination based on prejudice.

On the other hand, historical as well as recent studies suggest that discrimination may be due in part to economic incentives, in the sense that discriminators are able to realize economic benefits, directly or indirectly, by practicing discrimination, especially against those who are weaker than they are and therefore unable to fight back and inflict costs that would obviate any potential benefits.[8]

RELEVANT ECONOMIC PRINCIPLES

1. If perfect competition or perfect planning were practiced, discrimination could not prevail. Any material benefits from discrimination would be wiped out by competition or by plan. However, an imperfect market, imperfect planning, and segregated markets tend to perpetuate and aggravate differences in the realization of potential among individuals and groups, and inequalities result.

Implications: If economic discrimination is to be ended, controlled interference with the market is unavoidable so as to remove any potential benefits accruing from discrimination.

2. Underperformance or filling under-skilled and under-rewarded occupations by those discriminated against is sometimes explained by the principle of comparative advantage. Minorities and women are said to be best equipped to perform certain functions and thus acquire comparative advantage in those functions, which happen to be lower paid and little desired by the majority and by men. However, comparative advantage is based on certain production functions or levels of technology. Because ethnic minority and gender groups tend to be undertrained (underendowed) or occupationally restricted,

they end up with comparative advantage in the more labor-intensive and less capital-intensive activities, or with lower productivities and incomes than members of the ethnic majority or men.

Implications: By expanding training and raising levels of technology of certain ethnic and gender groups, the distribution of comparative advantage can be changed, probably to the benefit of these groups, as well as to the benefit of society as a whole, since production capacity will be increased and more incentives will be generated.

3. Equal opportunity is considered fair, just, efficient, and democratic. It is rarely specified, however, when the practice of equal opportunity should begin in the life of an individual. Equal opportunity would be more meaningful if it began at birth, or earlier, not when the individual enters the job market. Equality of opportunity becomes an impossible ideal if it does not begin until one enters the labor market. "In a time when the old barriers to blacks have fallen, when the doors of the establishment are partially opened, we are seeing that too many blacks can't even walk in the door," because they are unprepared, underendowed, and hence unable to take advantage of the "equal opportunity" concept.[9]

Inasmuch as affirmative action applies to the job market and education, it can be effective in dealing with the problems of discrimination and unemployment faced by minorities and women. It cannot, however, deal with the underlying deprivation of members of certain groups who have unequal opportunities and are unable to acquire sufficient endowment to be able to compete at an equal level upon entry in the market.

Implications: To equalize opportunities for minorities and women, economic policy should concentrate on equalizing opportunities to acquire endowments in the form of human capital (health, education, and welfare) from birth onward, [or before if we accept the psychologists' arguments that personality formation begins before birth of the child through the health and behavior of the parents and the social group].

4. Dealing with discrimination requires awareness and knowledge of the problem and its causes. Prejudice is largely based on ignorance and blind belief. Hence, one way to fight discrimination is to spread awareness and knowledge about discrimination and its effects. Advertising is a legitimate and often an effective source of information. It serves the consumer and the producer and raises efficiency in the economy by increasing both knowledge and choice and can be an effective instrument in dealing with discrimination.

Implications: Ethnic, racial, and women groups could use the spread of information as an instrument to acquaint the ethnic majority and men with their plight, reeducate them, and influence policy in favor of more equality and better targeting.

Suggestions for Students: Evaluate the extent and effectiveness of affirmative action in your home community. Recommend ways to improve its effectiveness if you think there is a place for it and there is room for improvement.

7

OTHER ECONOMIC ISSUES

Economic issues that relate indirectly to cultural diversity or ethnic composition of the population may relate to income distribution, consumption, investment, and growth or lack of it. Therefore, economic efficiency might be increased if policy makers paid some attention to the indirect effects on these groups, as follows.

1. Expansion of Exports: Export expansion may help the economy by increasing employment, financing imports, and improving technology. Restriction of imports could have similar results if full employment were guaranteed. Trade policy may be an effective instrument to achieve desirable results such as a balanced current account, but a blanket commitment to the expansion of exports, or to the restriction of imports, may be harmful to certain cultural and gender groups. For example, according to one study, women and minorities have been affected adversely by foreign trade policy, more than proportionally to their size in the labor force in the affected industries. Women were about 41.1% of the work force in the negatively affected industries and only 21.5% in the positively affected industries. Minorities were about 11.5% in the negatively affected industries and only 7.4% in the positively affected industries. More details are shown in Table 7-1.[10]

TABLE 7-1
CHARACTERISTICS OF WORKERS AND INDUSTRIES
MOST AFFECTED BY TRADE-RELATED EMPLOYMENT
CHANGES BETWEEN 1964 AND 1975

Demographic Characteristics of Labor Force (in percent)	Average of 20 Most Favorably Affected Industries	Overall Manufacturing Average	Average of 20 Most Adversely Affected Industries
Women	21.5	29.4	41.1
Minorities	7.4	10.1	11.5
Under Age 25	15.4	16.4	15.8
Over Age 50	24.4	26.5	28.0
Family Income Below Poverty Level	5.8	7.0	9.8
Annual Earnings Under $10,000	72.1	77.4	81.7
Annual Earnings Under $12,000	83.5	87.2	89.7
High School Education (4 years)	39.1	36.6	34.0
College Education (4 years)	6.9	5.1	3.1
Skill Measured as a Percentage of the Average Wage in Manufacturing (1973)	104.0	100.0	97.8
Skilled Workers as a Percentage of the Labor Force	55.8	50.0	38.8

Implications: To the extent that foreign trade may be biased in favor of higher-income groups who consume imports, producers who specialize in export products, and policy makers with vested interests, it may have direct and indirect negative effects on lower-income and lower-skilled ethnic minorities and women. Furthermore, in the absence of full employment, expanding exports to finance imports may be at the expense of domestic labor-intensive industry and employment, of lower-income consumer items, and of more urgently needed local and regional economic development.

2. Deficit Spending and the National Debt: The national debt is beneficial to groups that finance the debt and earn the returns from doing so. It is also beneficial to the industries and services that are financed by government expenditure and indirectly by the national debt. Given that most of the expenditure of the national debt is in highly advanced technology industry, and given that the creditors are mostly higher-income nonminority groups, the national debt may be harmful to the lower-income groups and minorities.[11]

Implications: Using the national debt to deal with problems of unemployment, discrimination, and inequality would be more effective if it were targeted toward the groups and industries that lag in the national economy. Furthermore, financing government expenditure by progressive taxation may be to the advantage of the ethnic minorities and women who are hurt by government deficit spending.

3. Underemployment and Low Economic Participation: Underemployment and low economic participation in general are costs to the economy. They are characteristic of certain ethnic and gender groups, either because of their cultural values or because of their lack of choice in the matter. In this sense, unemployed ethnic minorities and women seem like sources of economic cost to the economy while they are victims of under-utilization in that economy.

Implications: An efficient economic policy would identify the causes of underemployment and low participation among different groups and plan action to enhance participation by these groups, increase their choice, and guarantee full utilization and employment of all the resources.

4. Participation in the Market: Entry into and exit from the market are supposed to be choices made by the individual in response to economic forces. However, individuals and groups face differentially distributed facilities and constraints and therefore may have different responses to some forces. Ethnic and racial minorities or female groups tend to have fewer facil-

ities and face more obstacles than others; hence their rates of participation in the economy tend to be more limited than those of others.

Implications: Knowing the differential distribution of facilities and obstacles among different groups and their differential responses to policy will help refine the policy and make it more efficient. That, in turn, would reduce the vulnerability of ethnic or gender groups that suffer most from unemployment and the chronic threat of falling into the ranks of "discouraged" and "homeless." It would also reduce the losses to the economy.

Suggestions for Students: Identify the impact of trade on individual ethnic or gender groups. Find out why the "discouraged" are discouraged — by field work if possible. Debate the values of financing government expenditures by the alternative methods of taxation and deficit spending as they affect culturally diverse groups.

CONCLUSIONS

Understanding the general principles of economics is a prerequisite for understanding the behavior of the economy, even though the economy may not behave in exact accordance with those principles. Furthermore, understanding these principles is indispensable in predicting economic change, planning or influencing economic change, building expectations, and in trying to explain deviations from the expected behavior. Such deviation may be due to failure to understand the principles of economics, misinterpreting them, ignoring them altogether, or replacing them with other guidelines that seem more relevant, workable, and consistent with the objectives of the decision makers and other economic agents. Awareness of cultural diversity would help in explaining deviations from the norm, identifying the relevant guidelines or principles, and in making economic policy more efficient and effective.

In this Supplement, the impact of cultural diversity has been observed on various aspects of economic behavior, as reflected in the different behaviors of various ethnic and gender groups. The profiles of the different groups show significant differences in patterns of economic behavior and in decision making regarding consumption, saving, and investment. These difficulties lead to the proposition that modification of economic policy, fiscal and monetary, to target the specific problems of individual ethnic and gender groups would increase the efficiency and effectiveness of such policy in relation to both micro and macro objectives.

We have tried to isolate the impact of race, ethnicity, and gender on economic behavior regardless of economic class status. Discrimination cuts across economic classes and income brackets, although class and cultural identities often overlap. We have also highlighted the problems more than the solutions to encourage discussion and awareness, knowing that the solutions can be complex and painful. However, awareness of the problem and ability to analyze its economic causes and implications are basic steps toward the solution of the problem.

This Supplement offers just enough to scratch the surface of this subject and to stimulate awareness of it. It is hoped that students and instructors will consider these ideas and propositions as points of departure, both to enrich the principles course and to help solve persistent economic problems that are closely related to the plurality and cultural diversity of American society.

NOTES

1. *Items* 43, 2 (June 1989): 21, and William Ryan, *Blaming the Victim* (New York: Vintage Books, rev. ed.,1976).

2. Underendowment means less education, training, nourishment, and health care, or lower qualifications than the person is naturally capable of acquiring. Underutilization means less than full employment as well as below qualifications. Underrewarding means less returns to effort than the returns received by members of the majority or males in similar positions.

3. Broadus E. Sawyer, "An Examination of Race as a Factor in Negro-White Consumption Patterns," in George Joyce and Norman A. P. Govoni, eds., *The Black Consumer: Dimensions of Behavior and Strategy* (New York: Random House, 1971), pp. 250-256. More, however, is revealed regarding saving behavior in the next section.

4. James E. Stafford, Keith K. Cox, and James B. Higgenbotham, "Some Consumption Pattern Differences Between Urban Whites and Negroes," in Joyce and Govoni, pp. 275-287.

5. Marcus Alexis, George H. Haines, Jr., and Leonard S. Simon, *Black Consumer Profiles: Food Purchasing in the Inner City* (Ann Arbor: University of Michigan, Division of Research, 1980), p. 16.

6. *Ibid,* pp. 5-8.

7. According to Brimmer, there are differences among blacks with respect to holding risky assets. Young black women invest more in such assets than young men of the same income and age group. Andrew F. Brimmer, "Income, Wealth, and Investment Behavior in

the Black Community," *American Economic Review* 78, 2 (1988): 155.

8. Elias H. Tuma, *The Persistence of Economic Discrimination, Race, Ethnicity, and Gender* (Palo Alto, Calif.; Pacific Books Publishers), forthcoming.

9. Pete Hamill, "Breaking the Silence. A Letter to a Black Friend," *Esquire* (March 1989): 96.

10. C. Michael Aho and James A. Orr, "Trade-Sensitive Employment: Who are the Affected Workers?" *Monthly Labor Review*, 104, 2 (February 1981): 29-35.

11. See Tables 4-1 and 4-2 for the distribution of asset ownership.

BIBLIOGRAPHY

Aho, Michael C., and James A. Orr, "Trade-Sensitive Employment: Who are the Affected Workers?" *Monthly Labor Review* 104, 2 (February 1981): 15-28.

Alexis, Marcus, George H. Haines, Jr., and Leonard S. Simon, *Black Consumer Profiles: Food Purchasing in the Inner City.* Ann Arbor: University of Michigan, Division of Research, 1980.

America, Richard F. (ed.), *The Wealth of Races: The Present Value Benefits from Past Injustices.* New York: Greenwood Press, 1990.

Bowers, Norman, "Have Employment Patterns in Recessions Changed?" *Monthly Labor Review* 104, 2 (February 1981): 29-35.

Braun, Denny, *The Rich Get Richer: The Rise of Income Inequality in the United States and the World.* Chicago: Nelson-Hall Publishers, 1991.

Brimmer, Andrew F., "Income, Wealth, and Investment Behavior in the Black Community." *American Economic Review* 78, 2 (May 1988): 151-155.

Brown, Clair, and Joseph A. Pechman (eds.), *Gender in the Workplace.* Washington, D.C.: Brookings Institution, 1987.

Daniels, Roger, and Harry H. L. Kitano, *Asian Americans, Emerging Minorities.* Englewood Cliffs, N.J.: Prentice Hall, 1988.

Gardner, Robert W., Bryant Robey, and Peter C. Smith, "Asian Americans: Growth, Change and Diversity," *Population Bulletin* 40, 4 (October 1985).

Jaynes, Gerald David, and Robin M. Williams, Jr. (eds.), *A Common Destiny: Blacks and American Society*. Washington, D.C.: National Academy Press, 1989.

Joyce, George, and Norman A. P. Govoni (eds.), *The Black Consumer: Dimensions of Behavior and Strategy*. New York: Random House, 1971.

Linden, Fabian (ed.), *Expenditure Patterns of the American Family*. New York: National Industrial Conference Board, 1965.

Lino, Mark, "Financial Status of Single-Parent Households." *Family Economics Review* 2, 1 (1989): 2-7.

Mincey, Ronald B., "Raising the Minimum Wage: Effects on Family Poverty." *Monthly Labor Review* 113, 7 (July 1990): 18-25.

Myers, Patricia M., "Minority Households: A Comparison of Selected Characteristics and Expenditures Contributing to Future Economic Well-Being," *Family Economics Review* 4, 2 (1991): 2-8.

National Center for Education Statistics, *Digest of Education Statistics*. Washington, D.C.: U.S. Government Printing Office, different years.

National Center for Health Statistics, *Vital Statistics of the United States*. U.S. Public Health Service. Washington, D.C.: U.S. Government Printing Office, different years.

Oliver, Melvin L., and Thomas M. Shapiro, "Race and Wealth," *The Review of Black Political Economy* 17, 4 (Spring 1989): 5-25.

Pitts, Joyce Mathews, "Expenditures of Black Households — Housing, Transportation, Food, and Clothing," *Family Economics Review* 2, 3 (1989): 8-12.

_____, "Income and Expenditures of Hispanic Households." *Family Economics Review* 3, 2 (1990): 2-7.

Ploski, Harry A., and Roscoe C. Brown, Jr. (eds.), *The Negro Almanac*. New York: Bellwether Publishing Company, 1967.

Tuma, Elias H., *The Persistence of Economic Discrimination, Race, Ethnicity, and Gender*. Palo Alto, Calif.: Pacific Books Publishers, forthcoming.

U. S. Bureau of Labor Statistics, *Consumer Expenditure Survey: Integrated Diary and Interview Survey Data, 1972-1973.* Bulletin 1992. Washington, D.C.: U.S. Government Printing Office, 1978.

_____, *Consumer Expenditure Survey: Integrated Interview Survey Data, 1984-1986.* Bulletin 2333. Washington, D.C.: U.S. Government Printing Office, August 1986.

_____, *Employment and Earnings* 38, 1 (January 1991).

_____, *Handbook of Labor Statistics.* Washington, D.C.: U.S. Government Printing Office, different years.

_____, *U.S. Department of Labor News Release* 91-607, November 22, 1991.

U.S. Bureau of the Census, *Fertility of American Women: June 1990,* Current Population Reports, Series P-20, No. 454. Washington, D.C.: U.S. Government Printing Office, 1991.

_____, *Household Wealth and Asset Ownership: 1988,* Current Population Reports, Series P-70, No. 22. Washington, D.C.: U.S. Government Printing Office, 1990.

_____, *Housing Characteristics of Selected Races and Hispanic Origin Households in the United States: 1987,* Series H121-87-1. Washington, D.C.: U.S. Government Printing Office, 1990.

_____, *Money Income and Poverty Status of Families and Persons in the United States.* Current Population Reports. Washington, D.C.: U.S. Government Printing Office, different years.

_____, *Money Income of Households, Families, and Persons in the United States: 1991,* Current Population Reports, Series P-60, No. 180. Washington, D.C.: U.S. Government Printing Office, 1992.

_____, *Poverty in the United States: 1991,* Current Population Reports, Series P-60, No. 181. Washington, D.C.: U.S. Government Printing Office, 1992.

_____, *School Enrollment, Social and Economic Characteristics of Students: October 1988 and 1987.* Current Population Reports, Series P-20, No. 443. Washington, D.C.: U.S. Government Printing Office, 1990.

_____, *The Asian and Pacific Islander Population in the United States: March 1991 and 1990*, Current Population Reports, Series P-20, No. 459. Washington, D.C.: U.S. Government Printing Office, 1992.

_____, *The Black Population in the United States.* Current Population Reports. Washington, D.C.: U.S. Government Printing Office, different years.

_____, *The Hispanic Population in the United States.* Current Population Reports. Washington, D.C.: U.S. Government Printing Office, different years.

_____, *Trends in Income, by Selected Characteristics: 1947-1988.* Current Population Reports, Series P-60, No. 167. Washington, D.C.: U.S. Government Printing Office, 1990.

_____, *U.S. Department of Commerce News Release*, CB91-215, June 12, 1991.

_____, *United States Population Estimates, by Age, Sex, Race, and Hispanic Origin.* Current Population Reports. Washington, D.C.: U.S. Government Printing Office, different years.

_____, *We, the Asian and Pacific Islander Americans.* Washington, D.C.: U.S. Government Printing Office, 1988.

_____, *Workers With Low Earnings: 1964-1990*, Current Population Reports, Series P-60, No. 178. Washington, D.C.: U.S. Government Printing Office, 1992.

U.S. Commission on Civil Rights, *Unemployment and Underemployment Among Blacks, Hispanics, and Women.* Clearinghouse Publication 74. Washington, D.C.: U.S. Commission on Civil Rights, November 1982.

_____, *The Economic Status of Americans of Asian Descent: An Exploratory Investigation.* Clearinghouse Publication 95, Washington, D.C.: U.S. Commission on Civil Rights, October 1988.

U.S. General Accounting Office, *Asian Americans: A Status Report.* Washington, D.C.: U.S. Government Printing Office, March 1990.